N for Network,
I for Internet VOL.1

Restrictions on Alteration

You may not modify the Book or create any derivative work of the Book or its accompanying documentation. Derivative works include but are not limited to translations.

Restrictions on Copying

You may not copy any part of the Book unless formal written authorization is obtained from us.

Are you too young to modern technologies and feeling like sometimes you can't even follow what is discussed on the internet? Or have you already seen some in school but are still feeling frustrated because there are still so many difficult languages you have never seen? In the modern digital era there are many new words and phrases popping up on a daily basis. These new language stuff tend to be flexible and way less formal. Still, they can become fairly easy to learn if there are straight forward explanations available to get you started. This is exactly what we have prepared for you here - plain-English introduction of the fundamental tech terms you need to know to survive the 21 century classroom.

This book focuses on network and internet related tech words and phrases.

*

Copyright 2017 **Tomorrowskills.com**.

log in and login

It means the "sign in" action. Normally you must have registered an account first in order to sign in. For example, you may log in with your email address and password to view your schedule.

The term login may refer to the credentials you use to sign in, particularly your login name. In most cases the login is your account name.

It may also indicate the sign in action. It is quite common for web pages to display a login button for you to click and proceed to logging in.

account

Most online services require that you first register an account in order to log in and use the services provided.

Account registration involves asking you to fill in a bunch of information and specify an account name for yourself.

log on and log off

Log on means log in.

Log off means "sign out". You usually do this when you are about to stop using the computer. See this example: I logged off so that John could use the computer.

lockout

This usually means "account lockout". That is, you are being logged off (which may be against your will) by someone who has administrative power over your account.

internetwork and vpn

It is a network of networks, with multiple physical networks interconnected by multiple routers.

A VPN Virtual Private Network can create a secure connection to another network so that no one can intercept. You want to use it to shield your browsing activity from prying eyes on whatever sources.

routing

This is a process that allows information to follow the appropriate paths and reach the desired destination. It works at the background and is totally transparent to you the user.

This process is a MUST if you want to access the internet.

router and cisco

This is the device that performs routing. Information usually needs to pass through multiple routers before being able to reach the final destination. At home you may also use a router, which can share the broadband connection among multiple computers.

This device is a MUST if you want to access the internet.

Cisco is a famous manufacturer of routing equipment. Many believe that it actually invented modern routers.

console

This term can refer to a network capable gaming device (a game console) or simply a combination of input and output methods (console input via keyboard and output via monitor). A router can have a console connection (they call it terminal emulation).

switching

It refers to the process of directing a signal or data toward a particular destination. It usually takes place in a local network.

When you have multiple computers on a network that are sharing data with each others, switching must be performed.

A switch is the device that performs switching.

IOS

When written as iOS, it refers to the mobile operating system created and developed by Apple Inc. exclusively for its own hardware products.

When written as IOS, it may refer to the operating system created and developed by Cisco Inc. exclusively for its own router hardware products.

NOS

Network Operation System is an operating system primarily for supporting client computers. It provides printer sharing, file system and database sharing, application sharing, network management and security ...etc.

NOS runs mostly on server systems.

.NET

It is a framework for software development framework. Microsoft offers this framework as a controlled programming environment where software can be developed. It is Microsoft proprietary. Some software require this framework in order to run. You can download it for free from Microsoft anyway.

bandwidth

This is a factor that determines the Internet connection's speed.

People often use this word to indicate the connection speed. High bandwidth means fast connection ... etc.

broadband, 4G and 5G

Nowadays this word usually refers to high speed internet access. It is "broad" because it can transport multiple signals and traffic types.

4G refers to the fourth generation of broadband cellular network technology that succeeds 3G. It is many times faster.

5G, however, is the way to go since it is many times faster than 4G!

connection and last mile

It generally refers to the successful completion of necessary arrangements so that your computer or device can access the internet or other types of network. A good and stable connection is usually speedy (a speedy connection).

Last mile refers to the final leg of the telco network. It is what delivers connectivity to the household end-users.

cable

Technically this word can mean many things. In the context of internet connection, cable connection is one type of high speed access, typically provided by the local cable TV provider.

Sometimes people use this word to describe computer that does not connect through wireless means.

cabling and fiber

Sometimes it refers to the transmission media of the network. Sometimes it refers to the act of setting up cable connections for a network.

In the context of internet connection, fiber optic connection is one type of high speed access. The speed is VERY VERY high.

So when some body says the network uses fiber, it usually indicates a connection speed which is way more than sufficient for normal use.

upstream

It means your data is going "up" - you are sending things out. Example: Data is going upstream.

This term is usually used to describe connection speed for data upload. Examples: The upstream speed is high. There is an upstream traffic.

downstream

It means you are downloading data - data is being sent from somewhere else to you.

This term is usually used to describe connection speed for data download. Examples: Downstream is getting real slow... There is heavy downstream traffic...

upload and download

Upload is the act of transmitting a file from one computer system to another. When you upload a file, upstream traffic is incurred.

Downloads is the exact opposite of upload. You can, for example, download a file by right clicking on its link and choose Save As. When you download a file, downstream traffic is incurred.

save as

When you click on a web link via the mouse's right button, there is usually a small menu popping up with the option of Save As. This option allows you to save the image or the file in question into your local drive.

Save as is an act of download.

ftp

FTP File Transfer Protocol describes a method of uploading and/or downloading files through the internet.

The term can be used to refer to the method or the corresponding software tool. It can also be used as a verb - you FTP files to and from the server.

HTTP

It means HyperText Transfer Protocol. It is the underlying "language" used by web for defining how messages are formatted and transmitted.

As a user you cannot control or modify how HTTP works.

HTML and HTML 5

It is Hyper Text Markup Language. It is sort of a simple language for describing the structure of a web page.

The building element of this language is known as markup. There are many different taqs for making markups.

HTML 5 is the latest generation. It is way more powerful – it is more like a full blown programming language.

link and anchor

Often being referred to as a hyperlink, a link may be in the form of an icon, graphic, or highlighted text. It is commonly used on web pages for linking to other files or objects.

Anchor link is a hyperlink that links to a specific spot on the same web page. It does not take you to another page. you always stay on the same page.

index.htm

The default file of a web site. It is called either index.htm or index.html.

You do not need to type it out explicitly when visiting a web site. The browser will automatically call up this file.

history

Your web browser maintains a list of the web pages that have been visited. This is called history.

cloud

Formally, cloud computing refers to the delivery of computing services over the Internet. For most users, the cloud provides storage space on the internet for easy access without geographical restrictions.

cache and proxy

With a browser cache, your web browser keeps a local copy of all recently displayed pages for faster revisit.

With a proxy cache, there is a shared network device that can undertake Web transactions on behalf of the users. It stores the content so that subsequent requests for this same content can be fulfilled easily.

latency

This is a factor that affects your Internet connection's speed. It describes the delays incurred in the network data processing. Low latency means small delay times and relatively faster connection, and vice versa.

Copyright 2017 **Tomorrowskills.com**.

backbone

Backbone is the part of the computer network that interconnects various pieces of network or smaller networks. It is an important infrastructure you do not need to deal with directly.

base station

A base station is a fixed point of communication (a cell site) for cell phones on a carrier network. Simply put, it allows mobile phones to work within a local area.

backhaul

backhaul describes the connections from the base station to the core network. Backhauling means taking traffics from the base station to the central network infrastructure.

wireless backhaul

It is the wireless communication infrastructure that is responsible for transporting communication data from the end user devices to the central network. You can consider it as an intermediate wireless communication infrastructure.

Mobile Backhaul MBH is just something which is highly similar.

service provider

Sometimes being referred to as ISP Internet Service Provider, a service provider is a commercial entity that provides you with internet access (for a fee of course).

client and server

To make things simple, just keep in mind an end user is always a client. A client always enjoys services provided by others.

A client can be a desktop computer, a notebook, a mobile phone or a pad device.

A server is a way more powerful and resourceful computer that is dedicated for providing services to you.

A regular user seldom needs to work directly on a server.

peer and host

A peer is a member of a group of computers. These computers are of the same level - they can mutually support each others (that is what we call peer to peer).

By definition a peer can act as both a client and a server.

A host refers to a computer or any other device that can communicate with others on the network.

Technically, a client computer is a host. A server is also a host.

hosting

It is a service that allows people to post a website or web page on the Internet.

Service provider provides hosting services for a fee.

Hosting is not limited to web services. There can be file services, mail services, and database services as well.

token

It may refer to the security token device that the owner carries to authorize access to a network service.

It may also refer to a special unit of data being passed through the network for traffic control or other purposes.

packet

It is simply a unit of information or data being transmitted through the network.

There are many tech details related to this term that you don't really need to know... .

network traffic

This term describes the data that is moving across a network at a given point of time.

There can be many different network traffic types.

protocol

It refers to the language the network speaks. Computers and devices can communicate only when they speak the same language.

hack

It refers to the act of intruding into (hacking into) a computer system or device by a hacker. When we say a system is hacked, that means the system is compromised.

Growth hacking is different - it involves the creative use of technology, analytics, and strategy with product development to facilitate business growth.

malware and virus

Malware refers to malicious software written with the intent of doing something bad. Virus is a form of malware.

A computer virus is a program or piece of code that can be loaded onto your computer without your knowledge. As a form of malware it can spread from host to host and can replicate itself.

hoax and zombie

It is a scam that is distributed to deceive and defraud recipients. For example, an email hoax is sent through email messages.

Zombie refers to a compromised computer. A zombie network is a collection of compromised computers connected to the Internet. Hackers use these computers to launch larger scale attacks.

encrypt

It is all about encoding information in such a way that only authorized parties can decrypt (un-encode) and access it.

Special software functions are required to achieve this. You cannot encrypt something yourself without the help of special software tools.

firewall

It is a network security device that monitors network traffic. It can allow or disallow traffic based on a defined set of security rules.

It may be a hardware or software, or a combination of both. Firewalling means the firewall is at work protecting your network.

text and chat

To text somebody means to send somebody a text message via SMS or other means (such as whatsapp).

These are similar:
To message someone
To sms someone

Chat usually refers to online chat, where multiple parties can talk to each others via SMS or other means (such as whatsapp).

Chatting and texting almost always mean the same thing.

IRC and chatroom

Internet Relay Chat IRC is a protocol that facilitates communication using text in real time. Instant messaging is a form of IRC.

Chatroom is sort of a virtual room where a real time chat session involving multiple parties is taking place.

Many tech supports are now offered in the form of real time chat room.

forum

It is sort of a virtual forum for discussions where participants do not have to be online in real time.

Tech support forums are pretty common these days.

SMS and messenger

SMS stands for Short Message Service. You may use mobile phone to send SMS. Desktop computers cannot send SMS though.

Messenger generally refers to software that can be used to text people. Most modern smart phones are equipped with this kind of software.

whatsapp and FB Messenger

Whatsapp is a messenger program for smart mobile phones. It uses the internet to send messages, images, audio and even video.

FB Messenger is a Facebook based messenger program for smart mobile phones. It uses the Facebook platform to send messages, images, audio and even video.

FB ad share

It means Facebook, a very popular social media platform. It allows users to post comments, share photographs and links to interesting stories.

With a Facebook share some body is sharing your Facebook post with his or her Facebook friends, with or without adding commentary.

Generally, a Facebook post can be shared on ones own Timeline, on a friend's Timeline, in a group, or in a private message.

FB like

Facebook has a Like button feature which allows users to show their support for comments, pictures, posts and statuses ...etc.

People are increasingly desperate for Likes in the modern days.

newsfeed

A newsfeed is list of newly published web content. People can choose to receive push updates for new content on a website by subscribing to it. On FB, News Feed is the primary mechanism that highlights information such as profile changes, upcoming events, and birthdays ...etc. FB users can specify if they want content from the people and pages they interact with.

tags

Tags are simple data that describe information on a Web page. They may also be used to identify images or text within a website as a category or topic.

In the context of FB, when you tag someone on a photo, you are effectively creating a link to that person's FB profile.

When you are tagged, the corresponding photo and FB post will show up on your wall.

metadata

Metadata is data that provides information (how and when and by whom the data, and the way the data is formatted....etc) about other data. Tags are a form of metadata.

timeline

It is a FB feature which is nothing more than a reverse-chronological display of your history on Facebook and other life events.

memes

These are pictures with words on them. There are often special characters that have been invented for memes.

On Facebook there are memes all over the place.

twitter and tweeting

Another very popular social media platform. It allows you to send short text messages that are 140 characters in length to friends and followers.

Tweeting is all about broadcasting daily short burst messages to the world via Twitter.

tweet refers to the short text messages sent via Twitter.

youtube and youtuber

Youtube is a website designed primarily for sharing videos. Users are allosed to create their own profile and upload videos. They can also watch, like and comment on videos uploaded by others.

A youtuber is a person who produces and uploads videos on youtube. The person may even appear in these videos!

Some professional youtubers have their own official opening and ending clips in the videos they produce.

channel and subscription

In the context of wireless network, a channel is a radio channel, which is something more technical oriented.

In the context of youtube, a channel is a video channel owned by a youtuber.

You can subscribe to channels that you like so that you can receive notifications whenever there are updates.

subscriber

In a newsgroup, a subscriber will receive news automatically via email.

In the context of youtube, a subscriber who subscribed to certain channels will be notified whenever there are updates made to those channels.

live casting and chromecast

Live casting involve broadcasting real time live video footage (continual live streaming). Many people choose to publicize themselves online this way.

Because it is real time, the footage can hardly be edited prior to being broadcasted.

Chromecast is all about streaming video content right to a TV. To be precise, it is a device that can even stream music and other types of media from your mobile device or computer to the TV!

multicast and webcast

Multicast is a communication mechanism, Communication is taking place between a single sender and multiple receivers on a network.

Multimedia contents are typically distributed this way.

A webcast refers to media presentation that is distributed over the Internet through streaming. It can distribute a single content source to many simultaneous recipients all at the same time.

pod and podcast

POD is portable media player which specializes in playing MP3 files. Certain models are powerful enough to be considered as multi-purpose pocket computers. iPod is a famous example.

A podcast refers to a series of digital audio files that you can download and listen to.

mp3 and mp4

Short for MPEG Layer 3, MP3 is a popular music file format. This format is capable of compressing music to very small size (uncompressed audio files are very large in file size) for easy storage and/or fast delivery on the internet.

MP3 is audio only.

To make things easy, just think of MP4 as a variation of MP3 that can support video contents!

MP4 files can be distributed over the internet via streaming.

streaming

With this technology, a video/audio file can be played ASAP before the entire file is completely downloaded. This minimizes wait time on the user side.

Not all files can be streamed. Also, special server side equipments are required to provide streaming contents.

blog

As a noun, a blog is a journal or diary that is published on the web. As a verb, to blog means to write blog. Information posted on a blog is known as blog post.

There is a blog for almost everything! There are lots of people who have personal blogs just about their daily lives...

posts

On a blog page there are usually posts that are listed in reverse chronological order. These entries can be clicked on and viewed in detail.

On a discussion forum people can usually post questions and answers (so to find solutions to problems).

moderate

Sometimes when you post something on a forum this post won't be displayed until it is approved by the forum administrator. This administrator is known as a moderator. The goal is to ensure there are no improper posts being published.

vlog

vlogs short for video blogs - blogs in video format. vloggers record and publish vlogs.

Most vloggers post regular videos to show what they are doing. These videos tend to be more action-packed.

blogger and microblog

A blogger is a person who owns and maintains a blog. The action of writing a blog is known as blogging.

Microblog is a type of blog in which users can post tiny pieces of messages in the form of text, photos, videos and audios.

The small messages posted are known as microposts.

tumblr

Tumblr is a microblogging and social networking website. With it, users can post multimedia contents in the form of very short blogs.

Blogs can be "followed". Those who follow blogs will be notified whenever updates are made.

attachment and attach

Attachment refers to a file being sent together with your email/text message. The file can be of whatever format you like.

Some attachments are malicious!

Attach refers to the act of attaching a file. You may attach a file to email message, or to other text messages as long as allowed by the messenger programs.

PDF and acrobat

Portable document format, a very popular file type for documents. It is supposed to be readable on almost all computers and devices.

Commonly used as attachment.

Acrobat refers to the program that reads PDF files.

Acrobat has a PDF reader program which is free across most platforms. It also has a full suite which can create PDF files.

apps and apk

An app is an application software designed specifically for mobile devices. For example to browse media files on your network you need to have an app that can search for and browse these files. Mobile games are apps as well.

Since Windows 8, certain apps can run on desktop computers as well.

APK is the file format of android apps.

android

It is a mobile operating system. It is developed by Google primarily for touchscreen capable mobile devices.

Nowadays Androids can run on TV set-top boxes, laptop computers, and even model robots.

google and google play

Nowadays when you say "you google something" that means you use the google search engine to search for something on the web.

Google Play was known as Android Market. It is the digital distribution service operated officially by Google.

steam

Steam is a video game digital distribution service that provides gamers with installation and automatic updates.

It is cross platform. It supports PC games, XBox games, PS4 games ...etc.

END OF BOOK

*Please email your questions and comments
to admin@Tomorrowskills.com.*

www.ingramcontent.com/pod-product-compliance
Lightning Source LLC
LaVergne TN
LVHW052310060326
832902LV00021B/3798